Three Hundred and One Desert Haikus

(Dawn, Day, Dusk, and Night)

MICHAEL COOK

Copyright © 2025 Michael W. Cook

All rights reserved.

ISBN: 9798999392015

DEDICATION

Desert Haiku is dedicated to the country of Japan that gave the World the art of Haiku and to the Mojave Desert, the desert that inspired the content of the Haikus written in this book.

CONTENTS

Acknowledgements i

1 Dawn 1

2 Day 28

3 Dusk 55

4 Night 82

ACKNOWLEDGEMENTS

I would like to acknowledge all the teachers and college professors that taught me the English arts. Your contributions to my development nurtured my love of reading, and my eventual desire to share what I have written with others.

Dawn, the start of a new day, a new hope, and the fulfilling of a promise. It is the Earth waking up and prompting you to do so as well. Dawn is an inspiration and an epiphany if we allow it to be. Therefore, enjoy the dawn, embrace the promise of what the day will bring, and allow it to inspire your actions.

1. DAWN

1

**Clouds float between peaks
Sun comes over the mountains
A new day breaking**

2
Another day breaks
Bringing a new dawn morning
Life's eternal gift

3
Earth's smallest creatures
Survive day's heat and night's dark
Emerging with dawn

4
Dawn's inspiration
Day's deliverance of hope
Faith and love abide

5

Dawn's radiant glow
Beams of light shower the Earth
Heaven's emergence

6

The coyote runs
Satiated for the night
To the den by dawn

7

The dawn rain fragrance
Entices anticipation
And awaiting mouths

8

The asters and sage
Awaiting the break of dawn
To share their beauty

9

The Sun's first ray
Night's ultimate destroyer
Arrives with vengeance

10

The first crack of light
Night dwellers scurry to den
Day begins anew

11
Birds, flowers, and bees
Signs of life, Earth's new rebirth
Spring dawn exudes hope

12
Autumn, like dawn, breaks
A relief, a reckoning
Or Earth's next change?

13
Seek a new marvel
Closed minds miss the desert's gifts
Dawn's newest promise

14
The hungry come out
The first rays signal the hunt
Chasing survival

15
Purple and red skies
Color the dawn at first light
Desert's first warning

16
The plane flies at dawn
Taking to the sky, courage
History in works

17
The night's efforts done
Ready for another chance
Dawn awaits the Sun

18
Dawn's promise, high Sun
The challenge is accepted
History is made

19
Dawn comes, no warning
Soon, all that sleep will awake
Rubbing sleep from eyes

20
Orange ball of fire
The Sun ascends in the sky
Burning night away

21
Rays of light glimmer
Arrows of life returning
A desert bounty

22
The hare emerges
Fresh blooms from the rains await
Quickly, then safety

23
Sun-kissed rocks glimmer
Dew from the night shines silver
Sun-kissed rocks dull soon

24
Flakes of snow greets day
Dusting the ground one more time
A brief change of scene

25
The orange dawn thrives
Countless have brought the new day
Today is the one . . .

26
Night, misunderstood
No real relief at dawn, sigh!
Dawn brings misery

27
The road-runner's plight
Is it predator or prey?
It decides quickly

28
The bloom seeks the Sun
Searching for the nature's strength
Abundance of life

29
Brown, barren, empty
Life exists, survival reigns
Miracles occur

30
Desert sky invites
Explorers come join me now
Witness majesty

31
Give me a brief drink
Water will restore senses
A respite, calm, peace

32
Flowers, enticing
Tempting the bees to visit
Growth of the species

33
The daily promise
Daylight and a fulfillment
Sun across the sky

34
Excitement building
Spring, the birth of new season
Dawning of new life

35

Sunrise brings no heat
The Sun emerges, winter
Cold hardens the mind

36

Grant the day notice
Deliver a grand entrance
A scene worth seeing

37

Do not fear the rain
It lasts but moments, then clears
The Sun will shine through

38
Night's last grasp of dark
The Sun has always prevailed
Night shall come again

39
Light, then tall shadows
An explosion then the Sun
Soon the heat follows

40
Quails scurry in light
Their slumber interrupted
Their day underway

41

Hawks eye the landscape
The horizon offers prey
The hawk obliges

42

The breeze welcomes dawn
Inviting the Sun's return
And its dominance

43

The night hunt over
The Mojave Green retreats
To digest the meal

44

Come, view the bright Sun!
The morning awaits your eyes
And your attention

45

Hawks circle at dawn
Their attention on the kill
Coyotes watch on

46

The morning is lit
Sun casts its rays on the sand
And warms the cool Earth

47
The Sun comes to life
Joshua Trees come to light
The brown sands take flight

48
The silence of dawn
Softly announces the day
And the coming light

49
Rain comes before dawn
A brief relief before heat
And day's misery

50

Gnats swarm dying fruit
Even the smallest struggle
The cycle of life

51

Hazy, cloudy dawn
The Sun struggles to shine through
Yet still shines brightly

52

Dawn erupts in waves
First in bright light, then in heat
Then the passing time

53

The fire, long-since dead
It diminished in the night
And with it, the heat

54

Send the night away
Time for day's activities
The World comes alive

55

The timid hare waits
Sheltered by the desert brush
Watching the bobcat

56

A blink of the eye
The birds take to the new sky
Surprised by the dawn

57

Awake to thunder
The taste of rain in the air
Relief on the winds

58

Sandy battleground
The scorpions' final fight
To gain dominance

59

Crisp morning dawn air
Blows across the sands and skies
The Sun creeps above

60

Thorns give protection
The cactus hides the lizard
Waiting for the flies

61

Small prints dot the sands
Proof of life from night's journeys
Gone, not to be seen

62

Hawk eyes scan the sand
The new day will bring new prey
And a soaring dive

63

Count the skies' white clouds
Great marvels, the horizon
Float across the blue

64

Witness the first glow
The dawn's greeting to the World
Then, the grand entrance

65

The sky's great expanse
Unfurls across horizons
Coming into view

66

The lightning strikes first
Followed by thunder's great roar
The storm approaches

67

Sun highlights the view
A bright poppy field at dawn
Orange and yellow

68

The Earth's rotation
The Moon is driven away
Chased by the Sun's might

69

Snowfall greets the day
The rarest of visitors
That depart quickly

70

Desert's winter dawn
The cold, heavy air comes forth
Rejecting Sun's heat

71

The calmness inspires
Offering a peaceful existence
For the coming day

72

Bright yellow flowers
Prickly Pear's unique allure
Beauty, grace, and pain

73

Anticipation
The sunlight conquers the night
Bringing day to Earth

74

Eager for the light
Living souls crave the new day
Another journey

75

Dawn, the birth of day
Giving lives light, or taker
Not all dawns arrive

76

The final dawn breaks
The desert does not stop fate
One's last rays of light

俳句 Three Hundred and One Desert Haikus 俳句

The day. The entity we spend most of our waking moments. It is where we take in most of what we see, feel, and experience. The day can seem like an eternity, or like a flash of light depending upon the perspective that it is taken in. Day should be a gift of moments and experiences that enrich and add value to life. Live each day as if it is your last, for one day it will be.

2. DAY

1

Desert winds bring life
The fragrance of the new day
Rays of sunshine glow

2

The sand rides the winds
Blinding those that are present
Masking the beauty

3

Reds and oranges
Hues plaster skies above
Summer storms arrive

4

Flowers bloom, new life
Transcending nature's raw force
Inspiring courage

5

The road runner stops
Predator or prey spotted
Better safe than dead

6

The smell in the air
The familiar scent of rain
The promise of life

7

Life-giving rain falls
The dry Earth has been waiting
The return of spring!

8
The wind picks up sand
Taking it to fresh new ground
Mysteries of life

9
Desert heat warms skin
Validating the new day
The day's gift of life

10
The desert in June
Tranquility, summer breeze
Calm peacefulness, blessed

11
Summer, life giver
A new day for our World, awed
Creator of joy

12
The blue desert sky
Overhead, providing calm
Mojave summer day

13
The deepest blue sky
A wonder of Earth's blessing
A gift from the gods

14

The angry sky opens
Down pour the tears of the gods
Giving life . . . or death?

15

Rain in the desert
A welcome gift to the blessed
A curse to the damned . . .

16

Nothing is harsher
And nothing is more divine
A new desert day

17

Awe comes in all forms
Sands, heat, the flutter of wings
The crow knows Earth's wrath

18

Slowly count minutes
Days go slow, but pass quickly
Years flow like the sands

19

Thunder breaks silence
A cacophony of gods
Power from Heaven

20

A grain of brown sand
Look like all others to man
But they are unique

21

Look down from the rocks
Every direction the same
All paths lead to hope

22

How can it be day?
The night flashed and disappeared
Time cannot be stopped

23

The Joshue Trees
The desert poppies, the sage
Welcome the sky's rain

24

Barren, hostile, dry
The landscape promises angst
The faint of heart fail

25

The brutal midday
The Sun has no sympathy
Embrace its onslaught

26

The life-saving shade
Elusive and hard fought
Priceless and precious

27

The thirst for water
Day's sole constant companion
Sweat, or wait for rain?

28

Desert's oldest beast
The lizard embraces all
At home in the sands

29

Flies miss the danger
The lizard has mastered prey
And is off again

30

The rolling clouds come
Blotting the desert's blue skies
Promising relief

31

Industrious ants
Patrolling the desert floor
Calm impervious

32
An oasis, life
A magnet to all dwellers
Irresistible

33
Drifting sand footprints
Heading into sandy dunes
What is to be found?

34
Count the clouds again
Billowing white marvels, hope
What comes, rain or dread?

35
Mojave July
The Sun broils water from air
The day shows no end

36
Tumbleweeds and wind
The perfect desert union
Life's evolution

37
The desert's beauty
Bright asters bloom lavender
Desert coloring

38

The bee seeks the bloom
And the nectar stored within
The daily journey

39

Hazy horizon
Goes on as far as one's sight
Mirage, reality?

40

The heat on the skin
Warms the body from the night
Nature's mighty fire

41
May admiration
Astonishing allure, awe
Deserts can inspire

42
Beauty from the bleak
The bluest skyline on Earth
Mojave April

43
Wings flutter midair
The warm air provides the lift
The heat provides drive

44

The desert's oven
Radiant heat overwhelms
Crisping skin and soul

45

The lizard's head bobs
Its intentions become known
Will it gain a mate . . . ?

46

Raindrops dance on rocks
Beating a rhythm of life
Desert symphony

47

Desert soul, barren
Pure, crystal blue, deep crisp streams
Prone to drown, release

48

Nothing stirs, midday
The respite lasts so briefly
Soon, onward to night

49

Ants scurry midday
Flurry of activity
Despite the Sun's wrath

50
Visit the barren
Take nothing when you depart
Leave just your presence

51
Desert winds, brutal
Grains of sands scrub the hot air
The brave accepts pain

52
Desert's uniqueness
A furnace and a chill box
The dichotomy

53

Constant heat and light
Summer days, the Sun's bright rays
A buffet of life

54

Rain's scent overwhelms
The crows know what is to come
Staring at the sky

55

The truth is unfair
The desert's reputation
Centuries of tales

56

Sun-burned sand landscape
The winds lift dancing sand grains
Carrying them on

57

Mojave sky, fire
Spreads across the horizon
Scalding rocks and plants

58

Contrails mar the sky
Technology leaves its mark
Lines drawn in the sky

59

Shine, the Sun is king
No star is brighter, shine on
We await your word

60

The sky amazes
The land poses obstacles
Day, unforgiven

61

Who survives this heat?
Why must I endure this pain?
The desert welcomes.

62

One more minute, please
A drink of water suffices
One more breath, will do

63

Another breath, please
I do not want this to cease
Not here, this desert!?

64

Birds dot the blue sky
High above the burnt brown Earth
Soaring over man

65

Blue, white sky, auras
The wind is the only sound
Desert summer day

66

Cool breeze of autumn
Winds raise dormant tumbleweeds
Across the landscape

67

Ants swirl the entrance
Flurry of activity
Colony duty

68

Sun travels the sky
Bringing life to the surface
Spring erupts and thrives

69

Gangs of black ravens
Watch over the rocks and crags
Nature's vigilance

70

Breath in the hot air
The senses take in new life
Enticing the soul

71

The Sun overhead
Giver and taker of life
Moves over the sky

72

Shades of greens and browns
A field of Joshue Trees
Mojave's forest

73

The bluest of skies
Mid-day winds carry no sounds
Peace across the sands

74
Mojave's harsh Sun
Offers no solace today
Neither does the night

75
The path gives no clues
How long must the journey take?
What is at the end?

俳句 Three Hundred and One Desert Haikus 俳句

Dusk, nature's prompt. It is the universe's notice of transition from day to night. It signals the time for relaxation, enjoyment, sleep. It is also the Earth's way of transitioning from day to night, and from consciousness to slumber. Dusk can be beautiful to experience, or a wicked foreboding. Given the choice, make it a beautiful experience.

3. DUSK

1
Dusk, the death of day
A slow descent into dark
Night reigns over all

2

Calm sets with the Sun
The quiet breeze drowns all sound
Day slips into night

3

The last rays of light
Shadows retreat in darkness
Dusk graces the night

4

The setting Sun hides
Ducking below the Earth's crust
The promise of rest

5

More than barren Earth
The setting Sun is marvel
Night delivers awe

6

Day folds into night
Darkness engulfs the
Earth's light
Eyes close to all sight

7

Red streaks in the sky
The desert embraces dusk
A day's surrender

8

The infrequent breeze
A brief, welcomed luxury
And soon disappears

9

The lightning strikes twice
Announcing the coming rain
The day ends, night comes

10

The red Sun departs
Creating magic moments
That captures the mind

11
Peace exists at dusk
A good day ends with promise
Surpassed tomorrow?

12
Light and darkness meet
Nature's intimate ballet
Whisk off into night

13
The bird nests at dusk
Home in the Joshua Tree
Sheltering offspring

14
Day fights fall of light
Raging final rays of Sun
Failing to persist

15
Dusk drifts across sands
Covering the lands with dark
Like a cool bed sheet

16
A lonely footprint
What weight troubled the bearer?
So easily gone

17
Dusk arrives with rain
Rejuvenating the Earth
Drenching sand with life

18
Planes and Sun descend
Dusk harkens all to descend
Night is foreboding

19
Cold chases the Sun
Desert mountain dusk coolness
Fills the Sun's absence

20
Let me have your life!
The desert shall not conquer
Allusions of man.

21
Wings open and beat
The bat takes flight at sunset
Nature's pest control

22
The desert's Fuji
Rocks, not snow propel upward
Ascending Heaven

23
Wandering, an end
Sun finally sets, relief
Tomorrow's dread, wait!

24
The well-traveled path
Leads to and from all journeys
Even in the desert

25
Arid conditions
Breezes that boil the dry wind
Heat rises from the rocks

26
The strong carries on
The weak inherits the Earth
In fables only

27
Rage, the thunder howls
The lightening imposes fear
The rain beats the Earth

28
Dusk, a distant thought
The night now rules the dark Earth
Black silence til dawn

29
Barren lands hide life
Day's end signals adventures
Brave souls venture out

30
Rain hides the sunset
Missed in the blink of an eye
The day forgotten

31
Downpours drum a beat
Wildlife will fail to notice
Night awaits action

32

A brief retreat, dark
The moment is over, night
Hours before dawn

33

Red light retreating
Sliding over horizon
Hiding with the dusk

34

A shadow's retreat
Signaling the Sun's slumber
Giver of life rests

35

Mountains grow at dusk
Ending the sky's radiance
Eclipsing the Sun

36

Blinking eyes marvel
The colors of sunset awe!
God's bright masterpiece

37

Horizon, look on
Each day ends differently
Evenings amaze

38

The chill shakes resolve
Night offers little comfort
Winter's evening

39

The day was perfect
The end brings sadness and tears
The unwanted end

40

Blues and whites dissolve
Replaced by reds and purples
Nature's canvas art

41

Desert heat relents
The breeze brings evening dusk
Transition to night

42

The day's end, shadows
The Sun's last defiant stance
The last rage til dawn

43

The sparrow takes flight
One last view of the domain
Then the nest's safety

44

The roar of the Sun
Gives way to the calm of dark
Engulfed with blackness

45

Desert ground squirrel
Day's activities over
Retreats to the den

46

The Sun's slow retreat
Allowing darkness to come
And with it, the night

47

Day's death comes quickly
The Sun does not fight the end
And quickly gives way

48

Brief glimpse of beauty
Seldom witnessed in the day
Less so in the night

49

Rainfall quenches dusk
The soil eagerly drinks
Uncertain future

50
Silence blankets dusk
Wildlife takes in the last view
And resumes their plight

51
Darkness comes slowly
Inch by inch the shadows fall
The end brings the night

52
Evening breezes
The scent of blooming flowers
Carried on the winds

53

The fall of autumn
And the fall of today's reign
Offers new seasons

54

Walk into the dusk
Chase the Sun's radiant light
Finding the darkness

55

The sweltering heat
Does not get lost in the night
A permanent guest

56

The relief of dusk
Is a short-lived luxury
Darkness brings panic

57

Red Mojave skies
Paint the end of the spring day
Before the darkness

58

The brush gains freedom
The tumbleweeds race the wind
Nature's carefree plant

59

The scorpions stir
Seeking nightly adventures
Wary of others

60

Winds carry the day
Onward to its resting hour
The sunset, and peace

61

Colors paint the sky
A canvas for the artist
Earth, the first van Gogh

62

Pink and purple blooms
On the Beavertail Cactus
Give vibrant, sweet scents

63

The scent of sweet fruit
Brings wildlife out from hiding
Desert's rare breakfast

64

Temporary end
Day recedes, but does not die
Dawn's resurrection

65

Dusk ends unnoticed
The desert carries onward
Life, unstoppable

66

Dusk, the Earth's reset
A time to transition life
From action to rest

67

The pigeons fly off
Retreating to their safe perches
To wait out the night

68

The ground owl watches
Soon, the unsuspecting rise
To scurry, and die

69

The bobcat crouches
The hare senses the danger
Who survives the night?

70

Temperatures drop
As does the heat from the Sun
Winter night rises

71

Sunset, the great fall
The enormous core subsides
Giving way to night

72

The struggle for life
Begins with the night's darkness
Who will earn the dawn

73

Blacks and grays paint dusk
A deep darkness covers Earth
Until the dawn comes

74

Those that live will leave
Life shall perish into dark
Dawn's day ends with dusk

75

Darkness engulfs light
And lasts for eternity
The last dusk one sees

俳句 Three Hundred and One Desert Haikus 俳句

Night, the great mystery. We know so little about what goes on at night. It is our body and mind's rejuvenation period, our time to retreat within ourselves and experience our deepest thoughts and memories, the dreams that nourish the soul. Night can be a time of fear and anxiousness or a soft comfortable blanket. It really depends upon your perspective.

4. NIGHT

1

The sky's bright white orb
Hangs high above in the night
Darkness' knowing sight

2

Midnight, wait for light
Day shall bring resolution
Another new glimpse

3

Desert hills climb up
Closer to the night's dark sky
Moonlit silhouettes

4

Sun, cold, darkness, heat
What will be your downfall here?
You shall come to see

5

Give me the night, peace
Tomorrow I shall conquer
The dawn shall witness

6

Descending at dawn
Another mission, record
One more step closer

7

Rolling clouds, gray skies
Lightening rips the night silence
Rain plummets to Earth

8
The scorpion's fight
What is at stake, life, or death
Who lives tomorrow?

9
The silence prevails
Midnight in the desert night
Tomorrow brings noise

10
The night sky above
Its radiance brings new peace
And promise of dawn

11
Rainfall in the night
Missed by so many, sadness
Water washes doubt

12
The mouse scurries on
The night air promises food
The search for life's grains

13
Movement in the dark
The tongue flickers left and right
Night's successful hunt?

14
Cool air satisfies
One last respite before dawn
And the mighty Sun

15
One last drink, then sleep
The night succumbs to day's light
Slumber comes quickly

16
The peaceful night comes
The relief from the heat sooths
Small luxuries count

17

The desert sadness
Can engulf and overcome
Resist the urge, fight!

18

The midnight darkness
Sight defers to one's hearing
And the desert ghosts

19

Winter's bitter breeze
Creatures seldom venture out
Wait for the Sun's glow

20
The first thunderclap
The tempest awakes the night
And batters the sands

21
Snow falls in the night
It will be gone by the dawn
Desert mystery

22
Mojave's dark sky
Stars and constellations shine
Night's tranquility

23

Exquisite moonlight
Shines light on the Earth's marvels
Solitude and peace

24

The distance divides
Dusk to dawn, eternity
The nights seem endless

25

Cool night, bright moonlight
The silence rolls overnight
Cool, calm, peaceful sight

26

Sounds in desert night
Evoke fear, primitive fright
Pray for day's first light

27

The stars, Earth's bright lights
Deliver peace, calm resolve
And pure amazement

28

Man, engulfed by night
So small, insignificant
Stands alone, moonlight

29

Dusk to dawn, the night
So many souls interact
Day will never know

30

Dawn to dusk, the day
The fate of all determined
Night gives sweet relief

31

Crows caw with power
The night silence is shattered
Desert's alarm call

32

Huddled, dry but cold
The squirrels nestle til dawn
Waiting for the Sun

33

Cool November nights
Refresh the air and the Earth
Radiant new skies

34

Desert sky, promise
Can we achieve fate, and win?
Man's eternal thought

35

The strong can survive
If they can survive the night
Brutal darkness, dread!

36

Come see the night's hues
Majestic nature colors
A palette of life

37

Deserts never sleep
Mirages and miracles,
Many mysteries

38
Darkness blankets night
Moon's appearance is distant
Silence is present

39
The Sun's heat bears down
While the night rejuvenates
The desert's mother

40
Night lasts forever
Until the day lasts longer
The dichotomy

41

The night embraces
Wanderers of the desert
Providing solace

42

The night screams in pain
The lightening tears the night sky
Violating dark

43

The last wisp of smoke
Signals the end of the heat
Wake, or sleep in cold?

44

Start the campfire now
Night will not wait for action
Dark will descend soon

45

Campfire, moonlight, foes
Who shines the brightest tonight?
The viewer decides

46

Send the star across
Nature shoots the night's dark fate
Who witnesses fate?

47

Stars spatter the night
The careless artist was here
Nature's graffiti

48

Desert's distant Moon
Shines, illuminates, and awes
And leaves with the dawn

49

Once enthralled by night
Day pales by comparison
But returns daily

50

The guiding North Star
Navigational beacon
Or a distraction?

51

Coolness touches skin
Pushing the day's heat away
Rebirth of senses

52

At midnight, a new day
Nature's daily transition
Perpetuates life

53

The night comes alive
The desert floor, a highway
Ants cleanse the landscape

54

The barren sands, life
A single flower stands tall
Braving the dark night

55

The patient spider
Sits on the web seeking prey
Soon, the web shall shake

56

A small, brief glimmer
Dances on the horizon
Holding the night's eye

57

Waxing Moon's promise
A night full of hopeful things
Peace, calm, quiet, Earth

58

The passage of dusk
Brings the night stars into view
Capturing the mind

59

The flames dance lively
Offering refuge and warmth
Destined to fade, die

60

The waves in the sands
Slowly shift, changing landscapes
A new view at dawn

61

The apex of night
Alone with your memories
Provides clarity

62

Walk in the moonlight
Find beauty in the night's light
Soon it will be gone

63

The coyote trots
Seeking the meal for the den
The night will soon end . . .

64

Lost in the cool night
Wandering along game trails
Searching for the dawn

65

The death of the day
Gives life to the coming night
Ever so briefly

66

In the dead of night
A fight to the death ensues
A soul dies as well

67

The night stars sparkle
The desert's hidden treasure
Seldom seen at all

68

The desert's first birth
Deep within the Earth, new life
Soon to see the light

69

The stillness of night
Carries the calm in the air
As the desert sleeps

70

Moon's sliver of light
Offers the brief solitude
Of a World at peace

71

High in the night sky
Hangs the Moon's full majesty
Nighttime's emperor

72

Celestial forces
Moves oceans from high above
And minds from below

73

The dark weighs heavy
The body awaits shutdown
Succumbing to sleep

74

The dark, night stillness
Engulfs in tranquility
Brief moments of calm

75

All things are ending
The waning Moon, like the night
Shall soon end as well

俳句 Three Hundred and One Desert Haikus 俳句

俳句 Three Hundred and One Desert Haikus 俳句

Haiku. The Japanese short poem that follows the five syllable, seven syllable, five syllable format. For many of us, we were introduced to it in high school English class. You might have even had to write a poem in the Haiku format for an assignment. It is not as easy as you would think. The brevity of the five-seven-five format can be difficult. For me, I became fascinated with the art form. At that time in high school, I had no idea that one day I would live in Japan. Nor did I even aspire to do so. I never dreamed of experiencing the country and the culture that inspired and created the artform. I am glad I did.

Typical Haiku centers around the topic of nature, for which Japan has an abundance of topics to write about, being an island nation, with lush vegetation, ocean environments, and wonderful parks full of flowers. Each spring, inspiration blooms with the brief emergence of the cherry blossoms, and their quick demise within a few short days. The Japanese are the experts in the Haiku art form, but from them, writers like me have gained inspiration from the words shared by the Japanese poets. Hopefully, this body of work inspires others to read Haiku, and maybe even write it themselves.

俳句 **Three Hundred and One Desert Haikus** 俳句

ABOUT THE AUTHOR

MICHAEL W. COOK is a military veteran who spent eleven years in the country of Japan. As a fledgling author he has had articles published in the *Defense Acquisition Magazine* and has self-published *Are You Struggling to Keep from Drowning* and *Wrestling Dad*, both published in 2025.

He grew up in southeast Missouri with a deep passion for reading and learning. He holds an undergraduate degree in English from Chaminade University of Honolulu and graduate degrees in Management, Information Technology, and Engineering Management. He considers himself a life-long learner through both formal and informal education, which has been major contributors to his success in achieving his goals.

It was through his love of reading and writing and his experiences while living in Japan and in the Mojave Desert that inspired him to author this book.

www.ingramcontent.com/pod-product-compliance
Lightning Source LLC
Chambersburg PA
CBHW070853050426
42453CB00012B/2174